LifeLine

BIBLE STUDY GUIDES

♦ For Small Group or Personal Study ♦

BOOK ONE

Kurt Johnson

North American Church Resources
and
Review and Herald® Publishing Association
Hagerstown, Maryland

North American Church Resources provides materials for local churches in the United States, Canada, and Bermuda

Editing and Page Composition by Ken McFarland, Rae Patterson
Cover design by Helcio Deslandes

ISBN: 0-8280-0974-0

LIFELINE BIBLE STUDY GUIDES

Title	Topic

Book 1

1. The Bible—Can I trust It?	Origin and Use of the Bible
2. God—Who Is He?	Father, Son, Holy Spirit
3. Created With You in Mind!	Creation of Earth
4. Created for a Purpose	God's Plan for Man
5. Freedom in Jeopardy	How Sin Began
6. Jesus—His Identity	Understanding Jesus
7. Set Free!	Plan of Salvation
8. A Symbol of Freedom	Baptism
9. Called For a Purpose	God's Church
10. Guidelines for Daily Living	Ten Commandments
11. Obedience By Choice	Law and Grace
12. A Day With the Son	Sabbath—Part 1
13. God's Sabbath—Its Meaning	Sabbath—Part 2

Book 2

14. Signposts	Signs of Christ's Coming
15. How Will Jesus Return?	Second Coming
16. Death—Then What?	Understanding Death
17. Sin—Forever Gone	Millennium/Hell
18. Forever Young	Heaven/New Earth
19. Symbols of Salvation	Old Testament Sanctuary
20. The Future Predicted	End-time Prophecy
21. Symbols of Commitment	Stewardship of Life
22. Life At Its Best	Health/Lifestyle Issues
23. A Family Forever	Christian Fellowship
24. A Messenger for Today	Gift of Prophecy
25. A Spirit-Filled Life	Holy Spirit/Spiritual Gifts
26. Summarizing God's Message	Summary

Contents

Getting Started

These study guides are designed to be used in a variety of ways. You can study them alone, two people can study together, or they can be used in a small group setting involving three or more individuals. Small group Bible study can be both enjoyable and educational. The small group concept is not new—its foundations can be found in both the Old and New Testaments. The early church, in the time of Jesus and in the years that followed, was a community—a home-based Christian movement. Christian church buildings were virtually nonexistent in the Roman Empire until the time of Constantine.

The goal of these guides is for a group of interested people to meet in a home, public meeting room, church, or other location and study God's Word together. Ideally, the group will be three to twelve individuals sitting around a table or in a circle for an hour and a half to two hours, one day a week, studying, praying, and sharing together.

Often, group members come to the meeting from various religious backgrounds. Some may never have studied the Bible; this could be their first experience. Some may not know the location of Bible books or how chapters and verses work together. Others will have studied for years; they can assist those just learning.

Prayer, Bible information, and opinions will be part of the group discussion. Some group members may never have prayed out loud before. Others will be quiet and shy. Still others will love to pray and talk. Be aware of these differences. Never use pressure or put anyone "on the spot." All discussion and prayer should be voluntary. As a general rule, do not go around the circle for prayer, answers, or discussion. Allow for spontaneous, voluntary responses. This makes the group session more relaxed and enjoyable and allows for differences in personality and experience.

Three essentials to all group Bible study include:

■ Sharing (getting better acquainted with one another)

■ Bible study (understanding and learning about God's Word)

■ Prayer (applying what we have learned and asking God to assist us.)

The format suggested in these study guides is based on these three essentials and will be similar in each study. A brief description of each major section of the study guides is as follows:

GROUP LIFE

This section will provide an enjoyable beginning for your meetings. Each of the study guides will discuss the dynamics of what can make your group life stimulating. This subsection is called "Growing Together."

Also, your Bible study group should be a friendly experience. A non-threatening question to which group members may share their answers will assist them in becoming better acquainted with one another. This part is entitled "Sharing Life."

SCRIPTURE AND LIFE

Each lesson will also provide an introduction and background material that will shed light on the passages to be studied. As group members dialogue and compare one scripture with another, the result will be a positive learning environment.

Following the Scripture and Life section are three questions entitled "LifeQuest," which are the theme of each lesson. As you study the biblical material, keep these three questions in mind and then discuss them. The questions are:

■ What does this topic tell me about God?

■ What difference does this topic make in my daily life?

■ How does this topic help me in my relationship with Jesus?

APPLICATION TO LIFE

We must keep in mind that Scripture is not only for study but also for living. There are three parts to this section. The first is "Real Life"—an actual experience of someone who has struggled with the topic. The second segment is entitled "Your Turn," in which participants respond concerning how they are currently relating to the topic. The final part is called "Alone With God." This segment gives encouragement to each participant to do something during the week in his or her personal life in response to the topic studied.

As you study the messages in each lesson, Scripture will be allowed to speak for itself, as God intended. Experience has shown that the topics of this series, when examined and applied to life, will assist group members in finding fulfillment and meaning in daily living. May God guide you as you open the fascinating pages of His message for our day.

There are thirteen lessons in Book 1 and thirteen lessons in Book 2 of the *LifeLine Bible Study Guides.* You can study all twenty-six or adapt your study and choose just certain lessons—or even change the order! A list of the topics may be found on page 3.

May God guide you in your study, is my prayer!

—*Kurt Johnson*

♦ Lifeline Bible Study Suggestion ♦

Some members of your group may just be learning about the Bible—and how to look up texts in it—for the first time. Because of this, select Bibles for each participant to use during the study that are all the same, so that the paging is the same in each one.

I would suggest a modern translation such as the New King James Version (NKJV) or the New International Version (NIV). Some, however, may prefer the King James Version (KJV).

Before each meeting, the group leader should look up each Scripture reference in the selected Bible and jot down the Bible page number next to the reference in the lesson. This way, during the study members can look up each reference by page number. This will save time and assist group members not as familiar with the Bible.

1

The Bible—Can I Trust It?

GROUP LIFE

Growing Together—a Healthy Small Group

Simply bringing a few people together—without following a few guidelines—will not make for an exciting, well-organized, and interesting group Bible study. Several helpful hints for a group Bible study are as follows:

1. Develop an agreement (covenant): This is a shared understanding of the group's purpose and of the means whereby members will achieve their goals.

2. Form commitments: These are the guidelines the group is willing to adopt in order for its members to accomplish their purposes.

3. Be caring: Develop and nurture an atmosphere in which love and genuine empathy are available for each member.

4. Focus on life-changing content: Study of the Bible and reflection on the material learned will lead to knowing God and others better.

5. Communicate openly: This is the glue which binds members together with one another and with God.

6. Encourage openness and honesty: Expressing feeling is a part of life. Acceptance and love are key.

7. Uplift Jesus: A group can have a meeting without Christ being the center, but lives will not be transformed unless He is the focal point.

Sharing Life

As we grew up and went to school, our teachers attempted to assist in preparing us for life. Who was your favorite teacher? What did you like about him or her? How have you tried to be like that teacher?

SCRIPTURE AND LIFE

WHAT JESUS SAID ABOUT THE BIBLE

"It is written, 'Man shall not live by bread alone, but by every word that proceeds from the mouth of God.'"—Matthew 4:4.

As you study, be thinking about the LifeQuest questions:

■ What does this topic tell me about God?

■ What difference does this topic make in my daily life?

■ How does this topic help me in my relationship with Jesus?

No book has impacted the world as has the Bible. Some have died for it; others have attempted to eliminate it. The Bible's influence is not because of any inborn power of its own, but because of the source of power revealed in its pages—Jesus Christ, the Son of God.

The Bible is composed of sixty-six books, which are divided into two major parts. The first division of thirty-nine books called the Old Testament was written before the birth of Jesus. These books were originally written in the Hebrew language, with the exception of a few portions which were written in Aramaic.

The twenty-seven books of the New Testament were written after the death of Jesus and are the second division of the books of the Bible. The New Testament was written in the Greek language, which was the universal language of the Roman Empire. The Greek used was not that of the classical historians and writers, but the everyday language of the people called the "common one" or *koine*.

The books of the Bible were not originally written with chapters and verses. It was determined that chapters and verses would assist the reader in locating passages, and these were later added. Helpful as they are in locating verses, chapter and verse divisions often break the continuity of thought, making it important to read the passage in its full content.

Approximately forty writers, writing over a period of nearly 1,600 years, prepared their material, writing in the language of their day. God inspired their minds and guided their thoughts. A composite view of all the writers provides God's view of a particular topic.

❑ The Bible mentions several ways that God reveals Himself to men and women. Look up the following texts and discuss the points you discover in these verses about a) how God reveals Himself, and b) how that characteristic helps you to understand God.

◆ Nature—Psalm 19:1 _____
  What is your favorite nature scene?

◆ Human Relationships—Isaiah 54:5; 66:13_____
  Why is your best friend special to you?

◆ Jesus Christ—John 14:9_____
  What has Jesus taught you about God?

◆ Holy Spirit/Scripture—John 16:7-15_____
  How has the Holy Spirit or the Bible helped you?

◆ Personal Experience—Genesis 12:1-5_____
  How has God intervened in your life?

❑ In your own experience, what is or has been the most helpful to you in learning about God? Share why you marked what you did.

___Nature   ___Scripture/Holy Spirit
___Human relationships   ___Personal Experience
___Jesus Christ   ___Other_____

❑ What do the following passages reveal about the authorship and purpose of the Bible? What is their message to you? Amos 3:7; 2 Timothy 3:16, 17; 2 Peter 1:16-21

❏ When did you first begin thinking the Bible was a message from God? What are some of the questions you have about the Bible concerning who wrote it, its validity, purpose, or any other points?

❏ The word *inspiration* literally means "God-breathed." Scripture is God's thinking communicated to men. Describe what you think inspiration means and how it works.

❏ The following scriptures convey the message that the Bible is authentic and tell how it assists in daily life. Discuss the key points and their meaning.
   ◆ Psalm 19:7, 8 _____
   ◆ Psalm 119:105 _____
   ◆ Psalm 119:160 _____
   For further study: Matthew 24:35; John 17:17; 2 Timothy 3:16, 17.

❏ God has given instruction concerning how to study the Bible. Read the following scriptures and discuss what they say about Bible study. John 16:13; 2 Timothy 2:15; Isaiah 28:9, 10

❏ John 1:1-5 identifies Jesus as "the Word." What is the relationship of Jesus and God's Word (Bible)—both called by the same name?

❏ Why would a Christian study the Bible and pray each day?

❏ LIFEQUEST—Thoughtfully review these questions:
   ■ What does this topic tell me about God?
   ■ What difference does this topic make in my daily life?
   ■ How does this topic help me in my relationship with Jesus?

APPLICATION TO LIFE

Real Life

Jim was troubled. He was not sure if he could trust the Bible to be the accurate word of God. In fact, sometimes he even wondered if God existed. In his mind, Jim really knew there was a God—when he prayed he saw a difference for the better in his life. Jim also had evidence in his life that showed God had protected and guided him.

Jim finally did several things. He prayed and asked God to let him know whether or not God was really out there. Also, he studied the subject in the Bible, "Who is God?" (This will be covered in our next few studies.) Then he studied how the Bible came to exist.

After studying these topics and Bible prophecy in depth, Jim was convinced. He knew that there was a God who rules in the affairs of life and who miraculously directed the writing and preservation of the Bible.

Your Turn

Check the statements that most closely reflect your current feelings. (These are for personal reflection, not group discussion.)

___I am going to pray and ask God to guide me as I study this topic.

___I am going to study this subject until I am certain about my answer to the question concerning the validity and accuracy of the Bible.

___I believe that the Bible is the accurate and reliable Word of God.

___I am not certain yet how I feel about this topic.

___Other_____

Alone With God

If you have decided that the Scriptures are God's Word for you, then a daily study of the Bible will assist you in life. Don't, however, keep the truth about God's Word—as revealed by Jesus—to yourself. As opportunities arise, share with others what you have discovered. Ask your group leader for help on how to have a daily Bible study plan.

2

God— Who Is He?

GROUP LIFE

Growing Together—Love and Acceptance

Early one morning, Jesus stood in the temple in Jerusalem teaching the people who gathered around Him. As He talked, some of the religious leaders in the temple brought a woman to Him who had been caught in adultery. The purpose of these leaders was to trap Jesus. However, He instead used the situation to teach a valuable lesson. As the religious leaders condemned the woman, Jesus simply reminded them that they also were sinners. Jesus didn't condone her sin, but He accepted her as a person and admonished her to live a better life.

God does not ask any of us to force our lifestyles, habits, and opinions onto anyone. The work of the Holy Spirit is to convict of any change needed in a life. It is OK to have different opinions about scripture and life. Love and acceptance does not mean condoning or agreement. When I love and accept others without conditions, this means I am functioning as Jesus did on this earth.

Sharing Life

One day, in a discussion Jesus had with a group of people, He said, "The birds of the air have their nests, the foxes have their holes, but the Son of Man has no place to lay His head." As you think about places to live, share with the group the name of the town and state in which you were born. How long did you live there, and why did you move away?

SCRIPTURE AND LIFE

WHAT JESUS SAID ABOUT GOD

"You shall worship the Lord your God, and Him only you shall serve."—Matthew 4:10.

As you study, be thinking about the LifeQuest questions:

■ What does this topic tell me about God?

■ What difference does this topic make in my daily life?

■ How does this topic help me in my relationship with Jesus?

Have you ever been confused in trying to understand the identity of God? You hear terms such as "the Godhead," "Trinity," "Deity," "Father," "Son," and "Holy Spirit," and wonder how they all relate together. You feel something like when you have a 1,000-piece jigsaw puzzle spread out before you. Let's look at a summary of the preceding questions for an overall view of God, then study the pieces together.

The term *God* refers to the three persons of the Godhead—Father, Son, and Holy Spirit. They are called the Trinity, the Godhead, and other terms by various authors—though these terms are not found in the Bible.

❑ Read the following verses regarding the three persons of the Godhead. a) List the names of God, and b) the words that help you understand Him. Discuss the concept of the Godhead that is summarized in these verses: Genesis 1:1; Matthew 3:16, 17; Matthew 28:19, 20; Jude 20:20, 21; Deuteronomy 6:4.

_____

❑ The Bible discusses God by comparing Him to things we can understand. Which of the following biblical names for God is closest to how you understand Him?

___Shepherd (Psalm 23)   ___King (Mathew 25:34)
___Father (Matthew 6:6-8)   ___Husband (Isaiah 54:5)
___Rock (1 Corinthians 10:4)   ___Other _____

❏ Why did you choose the particular analogy you did?

_____

❏ The passages of scripture in this section discuss the attributes of
God. Choose two passages from each section to read and discuss
together. Briefly review the others.

Nature of God (Choose two passages)

■ God is eternal. Psalm 90:2
■ God is everywhere at the same time (omnipresence).
Psalm 139:7-12
■ God knows everything (omniscience). Matthew 6:8; Psalm 147:5
■ God is able to accomplish what He wills (omnipotence).
Daniel 4:34, 35
■ God does not change (immutability). Malachi 3:6

Moral Attributes (Choose two passages)

■ Holy   Psalm 99:9
■ Righteous   Ezra 9:15
■ Just   Exodus 34:6, 7; Revelation 15:3, 4
■ Loving   1 John 4:7, 8
■ Merciful   Isaiah 55:7
■ Truthful   1 John 5:20

❏ Which of the preceding characteristics do you appreciate most
about God? (Write down one from each section.)
Nature of God _____
Moral Attributes _____

Why did you select these particular characteristics? What difference do they make in your daily life?

_____

❏ If a Christian is to reflect God's life to others in actions and
words, which one of the above traits do you reflect the best? With

which one do you need assistance? Pray together about it.

___

❑ The Bible spends little time discussing God's physical appearance and concentrates instead on the Godhead's role in salvation and their love for people. The next three sections will give a glimpse at each member of the Godhead.

◆ **God the Father**
The Father's love is demonstrated in the plan of salvation in three ways—with the Son, with all men, and with Christian believers. Read the following texts and discuss what they tell you about the Father. John 14:1-11; 1 John 4:9, 10.

◆ **God the Son**
The Christian's understanding of Jesus' love is seen in what He gave up for us. What do the following verses reveal about the preexistence of Jesus? John 1:1-5, 14-18; John 17:5.

◆ **God the Holy Spirit**
Learning the identity and function of the Holy Spirit is an essential part of Christian growth and development. What do the following texts reveal about the role of the Holy Spirit? John 16:5-15; 1 Corinthians 2:9-11.

As you were growing up, what was your concept of God? Indicate below the answer that reflects that concept most closely. What made you think God was like the choice you made?

___A loving, understanding being   ___Santa Claus
___Impersonal and stern   ___"Out to get me"
___A power I didn't understand   ___Other_____

You undoubtedly have some unanswered questions about God. Almost everyone does. But one message about God is clear, and everyone can understand it. "Yes, I have loved you with an everlasting love." Jeremiah 31:3.

❏ LIFEQUEST—Thoughtfully review these questions:

■ What does this topic tell me about God?

■ What difference does this topic make in my daily life?

■ How does this topic help me in my relationship with Jesus?

APPLICATION TO LIFE

Real Life

Tom sat beside a lake in the park. It was a beautiful setting, but he was not focusing upon the beauty around him. His mind was in a whirl of thought as he tried to understand the Godhead. A friend's explanation helped. The term *God*, he had said, was like a person's last name. Just as there can be a father, mother, and child, so in the Godhead there is the Father, Son, and Holy Spirit. They are each God—and one in purpose and unity—but each is a distinct person, with a distinct role to play in the salvation of mankind. Tom eventually concluded that it was impossible for a created being to completely understand the Creator.

Your Turn

Because it is difficult fully to understand every detail about God, some quit believing in Him as Lord of their life. It is almost like saying, "Because I don't understand the principles of electricity, I won't use it!"

Check the statements below that most closely reflect your current feelings. (These are for personal reflection, not group discussion.)

___I am going to study this subject until I am comfortable with my understanding about the subject of the Godhead.

___I believe in the Trinity and that Jesus is divine.

___I am not certain about this topic or how I will respond to it.

Alone With God

Take time each day to pray and study the Scriptures in order to learn more about the type of person God is.

3

Created With "You" in Mind!

GROUP LIFE

Growing Together—Stages of Group Life

Most of us are aware of the stages of development in the life of each person born into this world. During these stages of growth from birth to adulthood, various patterns of development and independence may be seen.

Likewise, in the life of a Bible study group, the members will discover various changes and developments taking place among themselves. These changes occur as group members become better acquainted with one another. The stages are: (1) the leader gives guidance to the members, (2) members become comfortable with one another, and the leader is no longer the center of the group, (3) relationships are so close that the group almost knows how to guide itself, and (4) group members allow the leader to guide them because experience demonstrates that a group needs a leader.

Sharing Life

When Jesus wanted to spend time alone in meditation and prayer, He often went to a favorite location—the Mount of Olives. Share where your favorite place is to relax and unwind. What makes it special for you?

SCRIPTURE AND LIFE

WHAT JESUS SAID ABOUT CREATION

"For He [the Father] makes His sun rise on the evil and on the good, and sends rain on the just and on the unjust."—Matthew 5:45

As you study, be thinking about the LifeQuest questions:

■ What does this topic tell me about God?

■ What difference does this topic make in my daily life?

■ How does this topic help me in my relationship with Jesus?

It is common to hear people discuss the topic of creation vs. evolution or to read about it. The Bible, however, does not deal with this argument. The writers of the Scriptures are very definite in their view of creation. The Bible begins by stating, "In the beginning God created the heavens and the earth." Gen. 1:1. Also, Heb. 11:3 states: "By faith we understand that the worlds were formed by the word of God."

Volumes of books and educational programs exist in which man, a created being, attempts to describe how the world was made. The approach of this study is not to evaluate scientific data or theories, but simply to approach the Bible as a literal account inspired by God. This will be done in two parts—The Creator and The Creation.

The Creator:

As seen in the previous study guide, the unity of the Godhead would lead one to think that the Father, Son, and Holy Spirit would probably be closely associated in the work of creation.

❑ Study the following passages and discuss what is revealed about the identity of the Creator.

Genesis 1:1, 2 _____

John 1:1-4, 14 (To understand vss. 3 and 14, read John 1:1-18.)

Acts 17:22-28_____

Ephesians 3:8, 9 _____

❑ Explain the role of the Father, the Son, and the Holy Spirit in creation as revealed by the previous scriptures.

_____

The Creation:

This study is based on Genesis 1:1 - 2:7. To begin, read Genesis 1:1-5 (Day One). What does "In the beginning" mean to you?

___There was simply a starting point for creation.

___The world has existed forever.

___God was stating a point: He is eternal; all creation is not eternal.

___Humans cannot understand the term, because we are not God.

___Other _____

Describe what the earth looked like as God began creating (v. 2).

_____

Read verses 3-5. What item did God create? According to this verse, when does a day begin? When does it end?

_____

Read verses 6-8 (Day two). What items did God create?

_____

Read verses 9-13 (Day three). What items did God create?

_____

Read verses 14-19 (Day four). What items did God create? What is the difference between the light referred to in vss. 3 and 4 and that mentioned in this passage? _____

Read verses 20-23 (Day five). What items did God create?

_____

Read verses 24-31 (Day six). What did God create? What was man's job description, as given by God? What was man told to eat?

_____

_____

Read 2:1-3 (Day seven). What did God do on this day? What do the words "blessed" and "sanctified" mean (vs. 3)?

_____

❏ Read verses. 4-7. Was there a difference in how God created the birds, fish, and animals and how He created man?

_____

❏ How would your work week compare to God's?

___formless, empty, boring $\qquad$ ___good
___completed, fulfilled $\qquad$ ___restful
___fast-paced (full of moving things) $\qquad$ ___other_____

❏ Read the following list of the items God created. Which two are the most important to you? Why?

___light (day and night) $\qquad$ ___fish
___sky, sun, moon, stars $\qquad$ ___animals
___plants and trees $\qquad$ ___man and woman (family, friends)
___birds $\qquad$ ___sanctified, blessed seventh day

❏ Some believe God created the universe and then "turned it loose" to operate on its own. However, the God who created us preserves and maintains us. Read Colossians 1:16, 17 and Acts 17:28.

❏ What was the reason that God created man and woman and the world around them? What do you think are the "good works" that are mentioned? Ephesians 1:3-6; 2:10 _____

_____

❏ If you could tell God "thank you" for something He made that you enjoy most, what would it be?

❏ LifeQuest—Thoughtfully review these questions:
■ What does this topic tell me about God?
■ What difference does this topic make in my daily life?
■ How does this topic help me in my relationship with Jesus?

APPLICATION TO LIFE

Real Life

Carolyn was frustrated. She knew God had created her and all others to have a relationship with Him. But as a busy mother of two children, there did not seem to be enough time to pray and study the Bible.

She knew that taking time with God was vital to starting the day properly. She decided to get up a few minutes earlier than usual to read and spend time in prayer, although she was a night person. While the kids were in bed each evening, she spent quality time in Bible study and prayer. As she prayed daily and asked God for a continual filling of the Holy Spirit, she noticed a change in her attitude and spiritual development.

Your Turn

Check the statements that most closely reflect your current feelings. (These questions are for personal reflection, not group discussion.)

___I want to say "thank you" to God for creating the world for me
　　to enjoy.
___I know that God created me to have a relationship with Him.
___I desire to have a daily infilling of the Spirit.
___I desire to develop a daily schedule for Bible study and prayer.
___Other_____

Alone With God

Set aside time each day for Bible study and prayer. Everyone's schedules and needs are different. Do not compare your situation to others. The key is to spend time each day with God!

4

Created for a Purpose

GROUP LIFE

Growing Together—Sharing Questions

One of the reasons people knew that Jesus loved them was His interest in them as individuals. Because of His genuine interest in their personal lives, a special bond developed between them and Jesus.

In your study group each week, there are sharing questions to assist the members of your group to become better acquainted with one another. Do not be nervous about these times. Experience has shown that this becomes a favorite time for the group as they bond together. In fact, eventually most groups discover that the sharing time is too short.

Sharing Life

Childhood memories are varied for each of us. For every one of us, there were positive and not-so-positive experiences. As you think back to when you were in the sixth grade, share with your group where you were living and what you enjoyed doing most at that time of your life.

SCRIPTURE AND LIFE

> ## WHAT JESUS SAID TO MEN AND WOMEN
>
> "I have come that they may have life, and that they may have it more abundantly."—John 10:10
>
> *As you study, be thinking about the LifeQuest questions:*
> - What does this topic tell me about God?
> - What difference does this topic make in my daily life?
> - How does this topic help me in my relationship with Jesus?

Thousands of visitors a year make vacation plans that eventually bring them to the foot of Mount Rushmore in the Black Hills of South Dakota. In awe, they view the magnificent masterpiece created by sculptor Gutzon Borglum.

Some believe that Mr. Borglum's masterpiece in stone is the greatest of all sculptures. However, it cannot compare to the one God created on the sixth day of creation week.

All other acts of creation, God spoke into existence, but man was formed by God's own two hands. (Genesis 2:7.) God must have been excited to sculpt every detail of the first man and woman. What excitement He must have felt when He leaned over the clay form of Adam and breathed into his nostrils the breath of life! Adam and Eve had characteristics, faculties, and powers that clearly distinguished them from the other life forms of creation. These included reason, the power of choice, mental capacities, and aptitudes. Genesis 1:26, 27 says, "God created man in his own image."

❑   What does it mean to be made in God's "image"? Can any of His creation be "exactly" like God? If not, what do you think are the . . . similarities? differences?

❑   Let's study several scriptures to try and understand what it means to be made in the image of God. What was God's plan for mankind a) physically, b) in authority, c) morally, d) in relationships, and e) in freedom?

◆ **Physical Appearance**

The Bible does not provide many details about what God looks like, though it does indicate that God and human beings are somewhat similar in appearance. Read, summarize, and discuss the following texts. Do they give any clue as to what God looked like in heaven or on earth? John 1:14; Luke 2:4-7; Exodus 33:20-23; Revelation 1:12-16._____

_____

How would you describe God's physical appearance to someone?

___God and man's bodies are identical
___God is more muscular, taller, etc.
___I don't know
___The Bible is somewhat vague
___Other _____

◆ **Position, Authority**

Discuss man's role (as it relates to his position or authority) after creation. Compare this to God's role. Genesis 1:28, 2:15; Acts 17:24-29; Hebrews 2:6-8._____

_____

What do you think is man's responsibility to the environment and to other creatures?

_____

◆ **Relationships**

Man was created for relationships. Discuss what the following texts reveal about God/human and human/human relationships. Matthew 22:34-40; John 15:9-17; Genesis 2:18, 21-25; 1 John 4:7-11._____

_____

Who is one of your best friends? Why are they special to you? What does this friendship tell you about God?

_____

It is possible to love God and others properly if one has low self-esteem? What are some reasons for low self-esteem?

___not enough praise as a child
___being constantly criticized by a spouse, teacher, parent, or
    employer
___thinking your abilities are inferior to others
___other_____

What can someone do to have more self-esteem?

◆ **Freedom of Choice**

What do these texts reveal concerning Adam and Eve's freedom to choose and act? Genesis 2:15-18, 21, 22; 3:1-8, 19

_____

People have always had a choice about their lifestyle. Read Joshua 24:15 as another example.

_____

◆ **Moral Condition**

What do the following texts reveal about man's condition before and after sin entered the world? Genesis 1:27, 31; 3:2-5; Colossians 3:1-17; Ecclesiastes 7:20, 29; Ephesians 4:22-24.

_____
_____

❑ If God knew how mankind would be happiest—yet that their wrong choice would bring sin into the world—why did He create them with the ability to make wrong choices?

❑ Even though man was created in God's image, did he perfectly resemble God at Creation? Can a created being be exactly like God? Why—or why not?

❑ When you think about being created in the image of God, which statement most closely reflects your feelings?

___I am excited about it.
___I still do not clearly understand the topic.
___I wish God had prevented His original plan from being interrupted.
___I want to live as close as I can to the original plan today.
___Other _____

❑ LIFEQUEST—Thoughtfully review these questions:
   ■ What does this topic tell me about God?
   ■ What difference does this topic make in my daily life?
   ■ How does this topic help me in my relationship with Jesus?

APPLICATION TO LIFE

Real Life

"If God really loved us, why would He allow sin to enter our world? He could have stopped it, and we would never have known the difference. Think how much better life would be." Fred shared those words as he and Don discussed the subject of God's original plan for the world.

Fred had asked an excellent question—one that Christians have wrestled with throughout the centuries. Fred and Don came up with two reasons for God's actions. First, God wanted man to develop a moral character. In order to do this, man must have the ability to make choices. Morality could have been dictated or implanted into man's mind, robot-style, but then God's purpose in the creation of men and women would have been thwarted. They were created to glorify God and to have a relationship with Him, and a relationship based on dictatorial premises is not a relationship of choice.

Also, because of this relationship, God wants human beings to serve Him because they love Him, not because they are incapable of doing otherwise or because of fear. If created beings knew that the moment they "stepped out of line," they would be immediately destroyed, imagine the fear that would rule the universe. A relationship of love and interaction must involve the power of choice.

Your Turn

Maybe you are wrestling with the same issues as Fred and Don. You understand God's original plan for your life but realize how far off track man has come over the centuries. Disappointment comes to you as you realize what might have been. However, one should be encouraged. This story has a happier ending, as upcoming study guides will reveal.

Think about the following statements. Which of them reflects your current feelings? (These are for your own personal reflection and are not meant for open discussion.)

___I would like more information concerning the topic of God's original plan for man.

___The subject of man's original condition at creation is interesting, I understand the topic but I have some questions.

___I am thankful God created people with the ability to choose to love and serve Him so that fear does not rule the universe.

___Other_____

Alone With God

As you have studied this topic, you have probably noticed a difference between God's original plan and the way men and women are today. As we reflect on our own lives, we probably note a sobering contrast. Ask God to assist you in growing, during your lifetime, into the "true image of God."

5

Freedom in Jeopardy

GROUP LIFE

Growing Together—the Empty or Open Chair

Jesus wants to have a relationship with every person in the world. He asks those who love Him to share with others how wonderful a relationship with Him can be. One way to introduce others to Jesus is to invite them to your group Bible study. Many groups have discovered that the "empty" or "open" chair principle assists in this process. It works this way. During prayer time, place an empty chair in your circle, if there is not one there already. As a group, ask God to provide the members with opportunities to invite someone to the next meeting.

Sharing Life

Because people are created uniquely by God, they enjoy different things in life. What is the favorite task you enjoy doing around your house? It will be fun for your group to discover the diversity of responses.

SCRIPTURE AND LIFE

WHAT JESUS SAID ABOUT SATAN

"The thief [Satan] does not come except to steal, and to kill, and to destroy. I have come that they may have life . . ."—John 10:10

As you study, be thinking about the LifeQuest questions:

■ What does this topic tell me about God?

■ What difference does this topic make in my daily life?

■ How does this topic help me in my relationship with Jesus?

The newspaper headline screamed out the news. A rampaging hurricane had swept Florida and other southeastern states. Many were killed and billions of dollars of damage done as the storm wiped out homes, businesses, and other property. Families wept over their losses and asked, "Why, God? Why do innocent, hardworking people have to suffer?"

This same question has echoed through the centuries. Some writers have called the bigger picture through which the answer comes "the great controversy." The reason for this title is that God created a perfect world, as we have previously studied, but another created being in heaven interrupted God's plan. This interruption created a conflict or controversy about who has control over the world and whether God can allow people to live forever.

❑ Read the following passages and piece together the incredible events that took place in heaven. List the details verse by verse, then discuss together and write a summary of the account.

◆ Read Ezekiel 28:11-19. This passage discusses the King of Tyre, God, and the anointed cherub. Many call this an analogy and say it is referring to God and Lucifer. What does the word *analogy* mean? How does it apply to this passage? List the key details.

Verses 12, 13_____

Verses 14, 15_____

Verses 16, 17_____

◆ Read Isaiah 14:12-15. This is another analogy, using the King of Babylon as a reference to Lucifer and God concerning their conflict in heaven. List the details in each verse, and discuss the meaning of the events.

Verse 12_____
Verse 13_____
Verse 14_____
Verse 15_____

◆ Summarize in your own words the complete story you have gleaned from Isaiah and Ezekiel._____

_____

❑ Other Bible writers fill in details of the "rest of the story." What do these passages tell you about the result of the conflict? Revelation 12:7-12; Luke 10:18.

_____

❑ Lucifer yielded to the temptations of pride and the desire to be equal with God. He was not content with his identity and position. Many people are not satisfied with their identity or lifework. What would you tell someone who is struggling with these issues in his or her personal life? _____

_____

❑ The previously studied passages give several names for Lucifer after his fall. Some have also called him the serpent because of his approach to Eve in the Garden of Eden. Read Genesis 3:1-6. What was the temptation that caused Lucifer to fall, which he then used against Eve? _____

What phrase indicates that before the fall, God had discussed with Adam and Eve the results of disobedience (sin) to His plan for a happy, trouble-free environment?_____

_____

❑ The disobedience of Adam and Eve is called sin. In the Greek language of the New Testament, the word literally means "to miss the mark," in reference to hitting the bullseye of a target. Several passages that discuss sin are as follows:

- ■ 1 John 3:4   Sin is the transgression of the law
- ■ Matthew 12:30 He who is not with me [Jesus] is against me
- ■ James 4:17   If you know to do good and don't it is sin
- ■ Romans 14:23 Whatever is not from faith is sin
- ■ Romans 6:23 The wages of sin is death

These scriptures amplify that in their relationship with God, sin separates people from Him. Furthermore, this separation that first occurred when Adam and Eve sinned, caused man's perfect nature and lifestyle (discussed in a previous study) to change and become sinful. The result of this change was sin and death (Romans 5:12).

❑ Sin caused radical changes in man's previous situation. Read Genesis 3:7-19 and list the changes which occurred.

_____

❑ 2 Timothy 3:2-5 lists various traits in man's behavior that entered with sin. Which of them do you think are most prevalent in today's world?

_____

❑ The entrance of sin caused each person born on this earth to have a sinful nature. That is, humans are born with a natural desire or inclination to sin. Read and summarize the following scriptures that discuss this predicament of man. Romans 3:23; 1 John 1:8; Ecclesiastes 7:20.

_____

How do you feel when you realize the condition of men and women?

___discouraged   ___why try to be good
___disappointed   ___frustrated
___hopeless   ___other _____

Because of sin, Satan claims dominion of this world. This sounds discouraging, doesn't it? There is hope, however. God has not ignored the situation. In fact, His plan guarantees that sin will not arise again. Nahum 1:9 states that God will destroy sin, and that "affliction will not rise up a second time." What a beautiful promise.

❑ LIFEQUEST—Thoughtfully review these questions:
  ■ What does this topic tell me about God?
  ■ What difference does this topic make in my daily life?
  ■ How does this topic help me in my relationship with Jesus?

APPLICATION TO LIFE

Real Life

Sarah attended a meeting one night in the small country town where she lived. She was especially interested in two of the advertised topics: "Who is the Devil?" and "Where Will the Devil Spend the Millennium?"

Because her mother and father were spiritualists, Sarah had been raised to worship Satan. But now she was investigating both sides of the issue concerning the identity of the devil. She could tell stories that would make one shudder regarding the appearance of demonic beings in her home. The family even knew the demons by name. Sarah was feeling a need in her life for some other way besides the life she was living.

Sarah was caught up in a struggle between good and evil. Her decision would have to be radical in order for her to receive relief. As she attended the meetings, she learned about the origin of Satan and evil. She learned about God's plan for her life and that He alone could free her from the bondage she felt in her life.

Your Turn

Most people face the same struggle. The difference is that the devil disguises himself as he approaches people. In Sarah's case, he was more open because of the belief of her parents. Our choice is the same—will we serve God, or Satan? There are many ways that Satan seeks to win people to his side. It may be by certain TV shows, books, movies, friends, or work associates. In this life we are constantly surrounded by choices that place us either on God's side or Satan's. The decision to accept Satan's plan of deception or God's plan of peace and eternal life is critical, and it is the most important decision a person will ever make.

Check the statements that most clearly reflect your current feelings. (These are for personal reflection, not group discussion.)

___I have decided to follow Jesus.

___I need more information on this topic before I make a decision.

___Pray for my friends and family that they will decide to follow Jesus.

___Other_____

Alone With God

Sometime this week, sit down in a place where you can be alone to think. Ask God to help you analyze your daily life. In the things you see, say, and do, are there things that are not compatible with your relationship with Jesus? If so, make a decision, with God's help, to make a change in your life. Ask your group to pray for you as you seek to change. You do not need to tell them the problem area—simply ask for their prayers.

6

Jesus—Understanding His Identity

GROUP LIFE

Growing Together—Levels of Communication

People who have led numerous groups say that there are levels of communication that groups go through as members become acquainted and develop trust in one another. Level one is when the conversation is casual and centers around facts. Group members hesitate to share opinions or feelings. Commitment to the group sometimes is weak, and the threat level is low.

Level two occurs when members begin to use conversation that contains ideas and judgments. A commitment to the group develops, and meaningful sharing begins to be a part of group life. Level three is the ultimate goal of the group. At this level, conversation involves meaningful sharing. Commitment to the group is very high. One vital point to remember is that a member who has not moved to this level as fast as the rest of the group may feel a little uncomfortable.

Recognizing these stages and accepting the growth and progress of each member is vital to group cohesiveness. Surround your group with acceptance and bathe it with prayer, and enjoyable group life will be yours.

Sharing Life

People can have a profound impact on the lives of others. In your life, who, besides Jesus, has been the most influential person? Why?

SCRIPTURE AND LIFE

WHAT JESUS SAID ABOUT HIMSELF

"Jesus answered and said to him, 'If anyone loves Me, he will keep My word; and My Father will love him, and we will come to him and make our home with him.'"—John 14:23

As you study, be thinking about the LifeQuest questions:

■ What does this topic tell me about God?

■ What difference does this topic make in my daily life?

■ How does this topic help me in my relationship with Jesus?

One of the most intriguing topics of the Christian era concerns the identity of Jesus. Was He part God and part man? Was He fully God or fully man? Was He born just like sinful man, or did He have an advantage over humans? The following passages will assist in understanding the issues surrounding the identity of Jesus Christ.

❑ Jesus is called the Son of God and was born on this earth to Mary. Read John 1:1-5; 14-18. List and discuss the points that give insight into the identity of Jesus._____

_____

❑ Read Matthew 1:18-25—a summary of how Jesus was born (incarnated) on this earth. Discuss the facts you learn about the incarnation, or questions group members may have, such as, Who was the father—and who was the biological mother—of Jesus?

_____

◆ Verses 21 and 23 give two names for Jesus and their meaning. What do these definitions tell us concerning the purpose of Jesus' birth? For further study, read John 3:16; 1 John 4:9; 1 Peter 1:18-21.

_____

❑ Old Testament prophets predicted the birth and mission of Jesus on this earth. Choose two of the following texts to read, and discuss how these texts correlate with the New Testament account of Jesus' birth. Isaiah 7:14; 9:6, 7; 53:2-6; 61:1, 2; Micah 5:2.

_____

❑ An earlier text revealed that Jesus' birth involved both God and man. It is difficult to explain how infinite God and finite man can be united together in a single Person. In fact, Timothy calls it the "mystery of godliness." (1 Timothy 3:16.) However, the Bible does give us insights into the topic. Choose three of the following texts. Read the scriptures, listing under the appropriate heading the characteristics—either human or divine—that you find. Texts: Mark 1:24; Luke 1:35; Luke 2:40; John 1:4; John 1:29, 30; John 10:30; Romans 1:1-6; Philippians 2:5-11; Hebrews 13:8.

Human	**Divine**
_____	_____
_____	_____
_____	_____
_____	_____
_____	_____

❑ Jesus was born with human characteristics. He was "flesh and blood" (Hebrews 2:14). Paul, in discussing the nature of Jesus, described it in these words: "For what the law could not do in that it was weak through the flesh, God did by sending His own son in the likeness of sinful flesh, on account of sin: He condemned sin in the flesh." Romans 8:3. What do the words "likeness of sinful flesh" mean to you?

___physical appearance   ___same emotions as man
   like man

___human personality traits   ___sinned like man

___tempted like man   ___could have sinned

___became tired, hungry, etc.   ___other_____

❑ Paul, in 1 Corinthians 15:44-49, calls Jesus the "last Adam" or "second Man" (Adam). The first Adam was a sinner (by one man sin entered); the second Adam (Jesus) "was in all points tempted as we are, yet without sin" (Hebrews 4:15).

◆ If Jesus was just like man, how could He never sin?

_____

◆ How was Jesus "tempted in every point" as we are today? For example, there were no pornographic movies in His day—or automobile speed limits to violate. What then does the verse mean? _____

_____

The Bible describes Jesus' humanity as sinless. His birth was supernatural, for He was conceived by the Holy Spirit (Matthew 1:20) and at His birth He is described as the Holy One (Luke 1:35). He was the "only begotten son" (John 1:14, 18), or literally translated, the "unique" son of God. Jesus came to this earth with a specific mission. He came:

■ to demonstrate that sinful man, connected with God, can have victory over sin.
■ to pay the penalty of death for our sins.
■ to give us an "abundant life," in Him, on this earth right now.
■ to give men and women peace and hope.
■ Can you think of other reasons?_____

_____

❏ LIFEQUEST—Thoughtfully review these questions:
   ■ What does this topic tell me about God?
   ■ What difference does this topic make in my daily life?
   ■ How does this topic help me in my relationship with Jesus?

APPLICATION TO LIFE

Real Life

Sally and Pete were discussing the topic you just studied. They were attempting to pinpoint every detail about Jesus the God/Man. After much study, they concluded that there is much to understand and much that we cannot understand about God. It will be in heaven after the second coming of Jesus before some of our questions about God are answered. In fact, if a created being could completely understand the Creator, he or she would be—as Satan told Eve—wise like God. The subject is so intriguing that Peter says "even the angels long to look into it." 1 Peter 1:12.

Your Turn

As you have studied this subject so vital to man's salvation and which reveals Gods love, what is your response?

___I feel comfortable with my understanding of this subject.
___I would like to study this topic further.
___I want to express my appreciation to Jesus for His love for me.
___Other_____

Alone With God

Mark for future reference the passages of scripture in this lesson that helped you understand this important subject. As you consider Jesus' commitment to you, what will be your commitment to Him?

7

Set Free!

GROUP LIFE

Growing Together—Conversational Prayer

In conversational prayer, members of the group participate with short sentence prayers. Someone in the group begins, the leader closes the prayer time, and in between, members pray brief prayers, with members praying more than once, if they desire. This type of prayer avoids embarrassing anyone who may not wish to participate in the prayer circle on a given occasion.

Sometimes conversational prayer can follow the plan of praying in three areas—praise and thanksgiving to God, the needs of people outside the group, and for those within the group. The leader begins praying for the concerns of the first area, then pauses for sentence prayers. When everyone has prayed who wants to do so, the leader moves on to the second and then the third area.

At the end of the prayer, the entire group can read or recite the Lord's Prayer together. If someone does not feel comfortable praying but wants to participate, he or she can write out a prayer and read it during the prayer time. Remember that praying during the prayer time is voluntary.

Sharing Life

Jesus loved children. In the middle of a particularly busy day of preaching, healing, and talking to people, a number of mothers brought their children to Jesus so He could hold them and pray for them. The disciples of Jesus thought He was too busy for the children. But Jesus stopped what He was doing and took time for these little ones. When you were a child, what was your favorite game?

SCRIPTURE AND LIFE

WHAT JESUS SAID ABOUT LIVING FOREVER

"For God so loved the world that He gave His only begotten Son, that whoever believes in Him should not perish but have everlasting life."—John 3:16

As you study, be thinking about the LifeQuest questions:

■ What does this topic tell me about God?

■ What difference does this topic make in my daily life?

■ How does this topic help me in my relationship with Jesus?

On a hot, humid day, a young law student named Martin Luther trudged along a country road leading to the German village of Stotterheim. Suddenly, without warning, the sky became overcast, and a torrential rain poured down upon him. As thunder rocked the countryside and lightning zig-zagged across the heavens, a lone bolt of lightning sent the student reeling to the ground. In terror, Martin Luther called out for God to help him. He vowed that if he got out of this experience alive, he would serve God.

Martin Luther kept his promise. In the monastery as a new monk, he zealously tried to rid himself of sin and save his soul by his own good works. In frustration and anguish, he discovered that the harder he tried to overcome sin, the worse he felt. Finally, in desperation for peace in his life, Martin Luther discovered the message of this study guide.

Sin, in simple terms, is a separation between God and you and me. However, Jesus came to this earth to restore the God/man relationship. This is called the plan of salvation.

❏ Before we study this plan, consider two questions for personal reflection. (These questions are not meant for discussion.)

◆ Have you come to the place in your life that you have

the assurance of eternal life? ___ yes ___ no ___ not sure

◆ How, in your opinion, does a person receive eternal life?
What must one do to live eternally? _____

_____

❑ To understand God's plan of salvation, let's consider it in four
parts:

Part One—God's Plan

■ God loves you so much that He has a special purpose or plan
for your life. Read the following texts and discuss what you
believe to be God's desire for you. Romans 5:1; John 3:16, 17;
John 10:10._____

_____

■ What does this say to you about God's attitude toward the
people of the world?_____

_____

Part Two—the Problem

■ God gave men and women a will and freedom of choice.
When one chooses not to have a relationship with God, it creates a
problem. Read the following texts, then write down and discuss
the problems sin creates. Isaiah 59:2; Romans 3:23; 6:23.

_____

■ Through the years, many people have made attempts to bridge
the gap sin creates between man and God, but without success.
Read the following scriptures about man's attempts to bridge the
gap. Proverbs 14:12; Ephesians. 2:8, 9.

Which of the following do you think include man's attempts?

___job   ___Christianity   ___children
___family   ___sports   ___position
___money   ___new house   ___other_____

Part Three—the Solution

■ Read the following texts and discuss the solution to the sin problem. 1 Timothy 2:5; Romans 5:8; Luke 23:33, 46; Luke 24:2, 3, 7, 50-53; 1 Peter 3:18.

Part Four—Our Part

■ These are the steps to receiving Jesus into your life. Read these texts and discuss the significance and meaning of the key words in each passage.

1 John 1:9; Acts 3:19	ADMIT your sins; be willing to change
Ephesians 2:8, 9	BELIEVE that Jesus died for you on the cross, rose from the grave, ascended to heaven, and won the victory for you.
Revelation 3:20	COME to Jesus in prayer, invite Him into your life, and ask Him to control your life through the Holy Spirit.

❑ You can receive Jesus any time through prayer. Prayer is simply talking with God as to a friend. Here is a suggested prayer.

Dear God,
I know that I am a sinner and need You. I am sorry for my sins and ask You to forgive me. I believe You died for my sins. I give You my life and receive You as Saviour and Lord. Make me the kind of person You want me to be. Thank You for hearing me and helping me to follow Jesus. I ask this in the name of Jesus. Amen.

Does this prayer express the desire of your heart? If it does, pray this prayer, and Jesus will come into your life as He has promised.

❑ God's Assurance

■ *Are your sins forgiven?*
You asked . . . He promised. "If we confess our sins He is faithful and just and will forgive us our sins . . ." 1 John 1:9.

■ *Is Jesus in your life right now?*
You asked . . . He promised. "I will come in . . ." Revelation 3:20.

■ *Are you a child of God?*
He promised. "Yet to all who receive Him, to those who believed in His name, He gave the right to become the children of God." John 1:12

■ *Do you have eternal life?*
"He who has the son has life; . . .These things I have written to you who believe in the name of the Son of God, that you may know you have eternal life." 1 John 5:12, 13.

❑ LIFEQUEST—Thoughtfully review these questions:

■ What does this topic tell me about God?

■ What difference does this topic make in my daily life?

■ How does this topic help me in my relationship with Jesus?

Note: If you accept Jesus as your Saviour, then daily Bible study and prayer is an essential part of Christian growth. Ask your group leader for assistance on how to develop a daily study/prayer time with God.

APPLICATION TO LIFE

Real Life

Joan sat with a surprised look on her face. She had just finished listening to a television program talking about how a person can become a Christian. It seemed too easy to her. The speaker had read a passage from the Bible in Ephesians that said salvation was a free gift from God and was dependent upon Jesus.

Several nights later, after some discussion in a Bible study group, Joan was able to understand and accept that salvation was indeed a free gift from God and that her part was to reach out in faith and accept what Jesus had done for her. Joan also understood that "good works" or obedience, as it is sometimes called, occurred in the Christian life not in order to earn salvation but as a response of love to God.

Your Turn

Maybe you have always believed that a person must fulfill a checklist of items in order to have salvation. Possibly you have attempted to be a Christian but struggled with trying to meet the demands of the list that, to you, was impossible to fulfill.

Is obedience to God's Word part of the Christian life? Yes. But one must remember that obedience is not the first step. The first step is accepting the free gift of Jesus, which is forgiveness, cleansing, and His acceptance. Then He gives you power to follow Him.

Check the statements that most closely reflect your current feelings. (These are for personal reflection, not group discussion.)

___I accept Jesus as my personal Saviour.

___I am not sure if I want to accept Jesus right now. Please pray for me.

___I do not fully understand the plan of salvation. I have some personal questions I need answered before I am ready to accept Jesus as my Saviour.

___I once accepted Jesus as my Saviour, but later severed my relationship with Him. I now accept Him again as my personal Saviour.

___I have already accepted Jesus into my life and want to recommit my life to Him.

___Other_____

Alone With God

Through acceptance of Jesus, you will find peace and power as your life is filled with the Holy Spirit. Only as your life is filled with the Spirit will obedience become a positive and satisfying part of your Christian experience. Thank God each day this week for His free gift to you.

8

A Symbol of Freedom

GROUP LIFE

Growing Together—Group Interaction

One situation that thwarts positive group interaction is an imbalance in sharing by group members. Each group will have some members who have a tendency to be quiet and others who enjoy talking. If you are a person who likes to talk, that is OK—God made you that way. However, recognize this fact and make it a practice not to always answer—even if there is silence in the group. By remaining silent at times, you will encourage others to participate. If you are one of the quiet ones in your group, remember that your views and feelings are important to the others. Your opinion, viewpoints, and feelings are essential to the spiritual growth of others in the group. Also, it is OK to be quiet—God made you that way, but don't forget to share!

Sharing Life

As children and even as adults, many of us are intrigued by throwing a coin into a wishing well or pond. If you could ask God to do anything for you, what would it be?

SCRIPTURE AND LIFE

WHAT JESUS SAID ABOUT BAPTISM

"Go therefore and make disciples of all the nations, baptizing them in the name of the Father and of the Son and of the Holy Spirit."— Matthew 28:19

As you study, be thinking about the LifeQuest questions:

■ What does this topic tell me about God?

■ What difference does this topic make in my daily life?

■ How does this topic help me in my relationship with Jesus?

Many have asked the question, "What is the difference between Christianity and the other religions of the world?" All claim to have great teachers who encourage their adherents to be good people. Why do Christians claim that Jesus Christ is superior to the founders of other religions? One reason is that only Jesus has power over life and death. His empty tomb is dramatic evidence of that! The angel said to the women at the tomb of Jesus, "He is not here, but is risen . . ."

In fact, a religion that does not have an empty tomb and a coming King is not enough. Paul, the writer of the letter to the Corinthians, said, "And if Christ is not risen, then our preaching is vain and your faith is also vain. . . . And if Christ is not risen, your faith is futile; you are still in your sins! Then also those who have fallen asleep in Christ have perished. If in this life only we have hope in Christ, we are of all men the most pitiable." 1 Cor. 15:14, 17-19.

On the day of Pentecost after Peter preached the message of the birth, death, and resurrection of Jesus, the people in the audience asked, "Men and brethren, what shall we do?" Peter replied, "Repent, and let every one of you be baptized in the name of Jesus Christ for the remission of sins." Acts 2:37, 38. Why? To demonstrate that they believed in and accepted the birth, death, and resurrection of Jesus and His victory over sin and death for them. Acts 2:41 states, "Then those who gladly received his word were baptized."

A symbol of the meaning of being saved is baptism. Baptism has special significance to a Christian. It is a public demonstration of one's allegiance to Jesus. Have you ever wished that you could bury the past? That you could wipe out the mistakes and guilt and start over again? Baptism symbolizes how Jesus does this for you in your personal life.

❑   Read Romans 6:1-9 and discuss the relationship of baptism to the death, burial, and resurrection of Jesus.

_____

_____

❑   As one studies Romans 6, questions arise concerning the Bible's description of the method of baptism. In the Christian world today, various methods are used for baptizing. Some employ immersion, or dipping under water; others aspersion, or sprinkling with water; and still others effusion, or pouring water. Read the following texts and discuss any evidence that reveals how one is to be baptized.

Acts 8:26-40; Matthew 3:16; John 3:23; Ephesians 4:4-6._____

_____

The word for baptize in the Greek is *baptizo*. This word was originally used in the textile industry in reference to dying cloth. The material was placed in a large tub of dye and pushed under with a stick to be completely colored. The Greek Dictionary says *baptizo* means "to dip under water, to submerge."

❑   Read the following texts that describe Jesus' example and attitude about baptism and discuss the questions which are listed.

◆   Matthew 3:13-17:

If Jesus was perfect, why was He baptized?

_____

Why do you think John at first refused to baptize Jesus?

_____

What is the significance and meaning of the dove?

_____

(Further Study: Discuss the relationship of baptism and the Holy Spirit as revealed in the following texts. Acts 2:38; Matthew 3:11.)

Does a person receive the Holy Spirit before baptism? What did Jesus mean when He said His baptism "fulfilled all righteousness?" _____

_____

◆   Read John 3:5; Mark 16:16. What is the significance of baptism to the Christian? Is it optional? What about those who die before they are baptized—can they be saved? (Luke 23:39-43).

_____

_____

❑   The Scriptures relate certain criteria that should be part of a person's life as part of the baptismal experience. Read these verses, then summarize and discuss them. Matthew 28:19, 20; Mark 16:16; Acts 2:38, 41; Acts 3:19; Acts 8:36-38.

_____

Based on the information you discovered in the preceding verses, is there an appropriate age a person should be in order to be baptized?_____

❑   Some ask if a person should be baptized more than one time in life. Can you think of any reason for a person to be rebaptized?

_____

Some have said that Acts 19:1-5 reveals a guideline by which one would be rebaptized. Do you agree? If so, what is the principle?

_____

A promise! A person who accepts Jesus as Lord and Saviour of his or her life and is baptized belongs to the family of God. "But as many as received Him, to them He gave the right to become children of God."—John 1:12.

❏ LIFEQUEST—Thoughtfully review these questions:
■ What does this topic tell me about God?
■ What difference does this topic make in my daily life?
■ How does this topic help me in my relationship with Jesus?

APPLICATION TO LIFE

Real Life

From the time Helen was an infant, her family took her to church. She was faithful to God and committed to following Him. After her marriage and the birth of her children, Helen made it a practice to take her own children to church every week. God and His commandments were important to her.

Later in her life, Helen began studying the Bible to understand why there were different beliefs on certain biblical teachings among denominations. One area that she studied was the biblical teaching on baptism. Helen had never been baptized by immersion. As she continued to study, she realized the importance and necessity of being baptized by immersion. Helen was particularly impressed with the example of Jesus in demonstrating the need for His followers to be baptized.

As she contemplated baptism, she realized that she had a fear of water and of being up front in public that, for her, was a barrier. Because of this, Helen delayed her baptism. She prayed and asked God to take away her fear, but the fear persisted. Six months later, Helen still had not been baptized. One day she called her pastor and said to him, "Pastor, I am ready to be baptized. I cannot wait any longer. I am still afraid, but I have changed my prayer from 'Please remove my fear,' to 'Please give me strength.' I am simply going to trust God that all will go well."

A week later, Helen was baptized, and all did go well. She was content and happy in Jesus.

Your Turn

Do you have a need to be baptized by immersion, but you find that certain barriers stand before you? The barriers can be many. They may include a fear of going under the water, fear of being up front in public, a fear of what friends or family may think, and in some cases a change in a long-standing belief concerning the biblical teaching on baptism.

The more we concentrate upon our fears rather than on the promises and power of God, the more formidable these fears become. Satan desires it to be this way, but God has promised victory over fears!

Check the statements that most closely reflect your current feelings. (These are for personal reflection, not group discussion, but please inform your group leader concerning your responses so you can receive assistance.)

___I have never been baptized by immersion and desire to be baptized sometime in the future.

___I have been baptized, but because of circumstances in my life, I desire to be rebaptized.

___I would like more information about the topic of baptism.

___I want to be baptized, but there are obstacles that stand in my way. Please pray for me.

___I want to think about this and study more, before I make a decision.

___Other_____

Alone With God

Helen exhibited fear as she contemplated baptism. If you have the same feelings, or if you have other fears to deal with in your life, consider memorizing the following passage—Philippians 4:6-9: "Have no anxiety about anything, but in everything by prayer and supplication with thanksgiving let your requests be made known to God. And the peace of God which passes all understanding, will keep your hearts and minds in Christ Jesus."

9

Called for a Purpose

GROUP LIFE

Growing Together—Communication

Several factors contribute to a person's ability to communicate. Such factors include self-image, listening, and expressing feelings. If a person has a low self-image, other group members can assist that person by expressing positive feelings about what he or she says. Listening is another key item. Group members should give each person who speaks their undivided attention. In order for a person to express his or her personal feelings on an issue or text, an atmosphere of acceptance by the group members must be present. This is seen when members do not criticize others for their opinions.

Sharing Life

As you went through your day today—or in the time since your last meeting—did any particular event cause you to think about God? If so, what was the event or situation?

SCRIPTURE AND LIFE

WHAT JESUS SAID ABOUT THE CHURCH

"You did not choose Me, but I chose you and appointed you that you should go and bear fruit, and that your fruit should remain, that whatever you ask the Father in My name He may give you."—John 15:16

As you study, be thinking about the LifeQuest questions:

■ What does this topic tell me about God?

■ What difference does this topic make in my daily life?

■ How does this topic help me in my relationship with Jesus?

The word *church* is derived from the Greek word *ekklesia*. The original meaning has to do with any called gathering of people to meet for any stated purpose.

In the New Testament, the word *church* is used in several ways. Examples include:

◆ Christians around the world are called the church of God. 1 Corinthians 10:32; 12:28; Philippians 3:6

◆ A group of people in a community who belong to the same church congregation. Romans 16:1; 1 Thessalonians 1:1

◆ An actual gathering of Christians for worship. 1 Corinthians 11:18

Archaeological and historical evidence reveals that in the early days of the New Testament Christian church, there were virtually no church buildings. Church members met in homes. One example of this is seen in Romans 16:3-5, where Paul sends greetings to the church that meets in the home of Priscilla and Aquila.

The church, as understood today, began when Jesus called His twelve disciples and they began the evangelistic movement recorded in the Gospels and the book of Acts. However, Acts 7:38 refers to ancient Israel of the Old Testament as the congregation in the wilderness. The word used is *ekklesia*—the same word used for the New Testament church.

❑ Read Ephesians 1:22, 23; 5:22, 23. What does Jesus call the church? What is the significance of the term *body*?_____

_____

What does it mean for the church to submit to Jesus? What is your understanding of the message for spouses in this passage?

_____

❑ Read and discuss the parallels between secular and spiritual applications concerning the church in the following verses. Which analogy do you like best? Why?

A building—Ephesians 2:19-22 _____
A flock—John 10:14-16; Acts 20:28-30 _____
A family (children)—John 1:12, 13 _____

❑ Revelation 12:1-6, 13-17 describes God's church in conflict with Satan. The church is described as a woman, Jesus as a child, and Satan as a dragon. What does it mean to be the "remnant" (KJV) or "rest of" (NKJV) God's church? To whom do you think the verse is referring?

___Christians to whom   ___Christians of today
     Revelation was first written   ___Christians alive when
___Christians during the Dark   Jesus comes
     Ages and Reformation   ___Other_____
     who were persecuted

Verse 17 discusses two identifying characteristics of God's people ("rest of" or "remnant"). List and discuss the meaning of these two characteristics._____

Read Revelation 19:10. How is the testimony (witness) of Jesus related to prophecy? What is prophecy?_____

The Scriptures state that prophecy is a spiritual gift God has given to His people (1 Corinthians 12:10). Just as God sent a special message to Noah in his day and Elijah in his day, and just as John the Baptist prepared the way for Christ's coming, so it appears that God will give special guidance to His people before His second coming. Does it surprise you that God would guide His faithful people by the spirit of prophecy? Why or why not? _____

_____

❑ In describing God's last-day church, Rev. 14:6-12 discusses a message given by three angels. The message they bring is a message to be given by God's people prior to the return of Jesus to this earth. Read the messages. List and discuss the key points.

First Angel—Rev. 14:6, 7 _____
Second Angel—Rev. 14:8 _____
Third Angel—Rev. 14:9-12 _____

The third angel's message builds upon the first two. The world is called to true worship, informed that judgment has begun, and warned against man's devised forms of worship. Then the final angel warns against worshiping the Beast and his image and receiving the mark of the Beast.

Various interpretations of the identity of the Beast have been given over the years. One interpretation which many students of prophecy believe is taught by Scripture and history is that the Beast described in Revelation 13 began as the church-state union of the Roman Empire which dominated the Christian world for many centuries. This leads to the view that the image (Revelation 14) is formed when religion unites with the government to enforce its teachings and agenda on others. This will occur prior to the second coming of Jesus.

Two groups of people will emerge prior to Jesus' second coming. One group will follow man's teachings, which run counter to the Scriptures. The second group, as stated, "keep the commandments of God and the faith of Jesus." This group is sealed in the truth of Jesus, while the other is marked. Interestingly, both groups profess to be Christian and true worshipers of God.

Ask your group leader about study guides on the prophecies of Daniel and Revelation which will provide more details about the mark of the Beast and other prophetic messages concerning events to occur prior to

Jesus' coming. Read, study, and pray as you decide what God's message is in these Bible prophecies.

This study guide has directed us to many different Bible facts about the church. The following is a summary of what we have discovered.

- God's relationship to His people is personal and real. This relationship is described as a head and body, shepherd and flock, husband and wife, among others.
- God's people living at the end of earth's history are called the "remnant" or "rest of her offspring."
- God's people
  - ◆ keep His commandments
  - ◆ have the testimony of Jesus
  - ◆ preach a special message prior to Jesus' second coming. This message includes the hope of the gospel, the judgment, a call to worship the Creator; and a call to come out of false teachings and confusion to follow Jesus Christ.

❏ LIFEQUEST—Thoughtfully review these questions:
- What does this topic tell me about God?
- What difference does this topic make in my daily life?
- How does this topic help me in my relationship with Jesus?

APPLICATION TO LIFE

Real Life

Pete looked at Ward and said, "You honestly believe that God has a special message for His people to give before Jesus comes! I believe it doesn't really matter to God what people believe doctrinally as long as they believe in God and go to church."

Ward, however, thought that it did matter to God. He explained that there is a controversy taking place between God and Satan over who will rule the world and over the eternal destiny of mankind. Satan rebelled against God and was cast out of heaven. Then he came to Adam and Eve in the Garden of Eden and caused them to sin. Jesus came and paid the penalty for man's sin. Because of what Jesus did on this earth, He won the victory over

Satan and plans to return to the earth, destroy sin, and establish a new heaven and earth where He and His people can live together eternally.

As they talked and studied the Bible, Pete began to see that God has always had a group of people who have shared a unique message from God. In the Old Testament it was the Israelites; in the New Testament God worked through the apostles and their converts. Others have stood up and proclaimed truth during the Dark Ages and Reformation—people such as the Waldenses, Martin Luther, and others. Now, in the days prior to the coming of Jesus to this earth to end the great controversy of the centuries, Jesus has a final message of preparation to be given by His people.

Pete discovered that anyone who chooses can be a part of God's people who will share His final message. He decided to accept Jesus as Lord and Saviour and become a part of the group preparing the world for Jesus' coming.

Your Turn

As you have studied this guide, perhaps you have discovered that God has a special message to share with the world to prepare them for the coming of Jesus.

Check the statements that most closely reflect your feelings. (These are for personal reflection, not group discussion.)

___I have found this study to be interesting and intriguing, but I still have unanswered questions concerning it.

___I want to belong to God's church—that fellowship of believers who desire to follow scripture completely in their lives.

___I desire to use my abilities and talents under the guidance of the Holy Spirit to share the final message with the world.

___Pray for me as I continue to study.

___Other_____

Alone With God

During your daily devotional time, ask God to help you think of friends and acquaintances with whom you could share your excitement about the Bible. Discuss with your group leader how you might do this. In some cases it may be best simply to pray and ask God to provide an opportunity or opening for sharing.

10

Guidelines for Daily Living

GROUP LIFE

Growing Together—Prayer Partners

Jesus believed in prayer. Many times He prayed all night beside a lake, on a grassy hillside, on a mountainside, or at the house of a friend. Before Jesus returned to heaven following the resurrection, He prayed for His disciples. This prayer of Jesus is recorded in John 17:6-26. The prayer also includes Christians on the earth today!

Why did Jesus pray for Himself and for each of us? Because He knew that prayer was the link to God through which one receives strength to deal with life's daily challenges and stresses. Christians have discovered that prayer partners in a small group can greatly assist each other. The concept is simple. Group members divide into smaller units of two or three. The men pair up together—and the women together. At the end of the group meeting, the prayer partners get together for a few minutes to share with one another. During the week, they pray about each other's concerns. Group members discover that support and strength comes from knowing that others are specifically praying for them.

Sharing Life

Jesus' birth is a significant event for every Christian, and is traditionally celebrated on December 25. Share your favorite Christmas memory.

SCRIPTURE AND LIFE

WHAT JESUS SAID ABOUT THE COMMANDMENTS

"Jesus said to him, 'You shall love the Lord your God with all your heart, with all your soul, and with all your mind. This is the first and great commandment.'"—Matthew 22:37, 38

As you study, be thinking about the LifeQuest questions:
- What does this topic tell me about God?
- What difference does this topic make in my daily life?
- How does this topic help me in my relationship with Jesus?

The sin of Adam and Eve and their offspring posed a problem for God to solve. A Saviour was needed to save mankind from its sins, but God also needed a committed group of people to tell others about His love and the plan of salvation.

God chose the nation of Israel. The Bible states that God's plan for Israel included freeing them from slavery, leading them to a fertile land that was a fantastic place to live; and instructing them in civil, religious, and health laws so they would have an optimum society. The goal was that other nations, desiring the same lifestyle and blessings they observed in Israel, would come to learn more about Israel and its God.

The time had come for God to explain His plan to Israel and to discuss with them the kind of relationship with Him that would result in His promised plan.

❑ When the Israelite people arrived in the wilderness at the base of Mt. Sinai, God decided to talk to them about His plan. We read about the discussion in Exodus 19:1-9.

What does God expect from the people? _____
What will He give in return? _____

What right does God have to determine the conditions of the relationship? Is He being fair? _____
_____

What does it mean to be a "kingdom of priests and a holy nation?"

_____

❑ Exodus 20:1-17 describes details of the covenant relationship God wanted with Israel. This covenant is called the Ten Commandments. The Israelites agreed to follow the commandments because they loved God and realized that He knew what would bring them the greatest happiness. The commandments were significant not only for Israel, but also today for God's people as they make them a love response of their relationship with Him. Read the following verses and discuss the questions about the Ten Commandments.

Verses 1-3—What was a "god" for Israel? What is a "god" for people today?_____

_____

Does it bother you that God wants to be first in your life above wealth, friends, spouse, knowledge or position?_____

Verses 4-6—What is an "idol" or "graven image?" Does this command prohibit religious sculptures and paintings?_____

_____

Can you think of any religious artistry or representations used in Scripture? (See 1 Kings 6:23-26; Numbers 21:8, 9; 2 Kings 18:4.)

_____

Do you think God makes a distinction between religious paintings or objects created as works of beauty or inspiration and those that are used as objects of worship?_____

Verse 7—How do we misuse the Lord's name in action and word?

_____

Verses 8-11—When was the Sabbath first given to man, and why? (Genesis 2:1-3) What does it mean that the Sabbath is "holy"?

_____

Verse 12—What does "to honor" mean? What does this type of behavior look and sound like?_____

_____

Verse 13—We tend to think of this commandment as referring to the premeditated act of killing someone. Could it also include acts of injustice that shorten life, the spirit of hatred and revenge, a selfish neglect of the hungry and suffering, or health practices that lead to a premature death? _____

Verse 14—Jesus defined adultery as including physical acts, words, and thoughts of lust. Matthew 5:27, 28. How does Jesus' definition preserve the "one flesh" concept of marriage?

_____

When is a thought a temptation and not a sin? What makes it a sin? _____

Verse 15—Write a definition of stealing._____

_____

Which of these would be wrong, based on your definition?

___Robbing a grocery store at gunpoint
___Shoplifting
___Filing a false income tax report
___Being lazy at work
___Trading in a car with a bad engine and not telling the dealer
___Copying a friend's homework

Verse 16—Which of the following apply to this commandment?

___Telling a story you heard about another without verifying the
    facts
___Lying in court
___Lying to someone about another person
___Intentional overstatements made to affect someone's opinions

Verse 17—Coveting seems to be based on selfishness. How does this commandment relate to the other nine commandments?

_____

❏ Jesus was asked one day about which commandment was the greatest. Read His response in Matthew 22:34-40. Then a) discuss what you think Jesus meant, b) relate Jesus' statement to what you have just studied, and c) indicate what "the Law and the Prophets" referred to here means._____

_____

❏ In Jeremiah 31:31-33, God speaks of a new covenant with Israel in which He will "put the law in their minds and write it on their hearts." What does this mean? How does it relate to the Ten Commandment, to God's Word in general, and to one's relationship with Him?

_____

❏ LIFEQUEST—Thoughtfully review these questions:
   ■ What does this topic tell me about God?
   ■ What difference does this topic make in my daily life?
   ■ How does this topic help me in my relationship with Jesus?

APPLICATION TO LIFE

Real Life

"The problem with Christianity is that it is a list of confining do's and don'ts. There is always someone looking over your shoulder trying to tell you what to do and what not to do. I like to live my life in my own way—not according to someone else's design. Who wants to live by the Ten Commandments, anyway?"

So said Jim as he and his mother discussed the benefits of Christianity and church attendance. Jim felt the restrictions of God's law rather than its freedom.

Jim's difficulty with the law of God and church attendance was rooted in the fact that he felt forced and pressured, rather than doing right as the result of a relationship. In fact, many people despise church and have a distaste for religion for that very reason. Well-meaning friends, spouses, and parents try to force obedience to God's law upon others before they know and have accepted Jesus. This is like two strangers, or near strangers, getting married and trying to do special things for one another—including remaining faithful to a marriage vow—when love has not blossomed in the relationship.

Just as faithfulness and a desire to do good works toward a friend, relative, or spouse is based upon a relationship, so is obedience to the law of God. When people accept Jesus as their Saviour and love Him for what He has done in the plan of salvation, then the law of God becomes a vow or symbol of their relationship. Obedience then comes as a desire of the mind and heart rather than as an "I do it because I have to" duty.

Your Turn

It is easy to fall into Jim's situation and react against the commandments. For you, do the commandments provide meaning or confinement? Your relationship with Jesus could make a difference in your response.

Check the statements that most closely reflect your current feelings. (These are for personal reflection, not group discussion.)

___Right now, the commandments seem burdensome to me.

___Please pray for me as I continue to consider this important topic.

___I do not consider the commandments to be a negative part of life.

___I choose to follow the commandments in my life because of my relationship with Jesus.

___I realize that obedience only has meaning because of one's relationship with Jesus Christ. I desire to give my life to Him and to become a Christian.

___Other_____

Alone With God

It is easy to let the attitudes and opinions of others affect the way we think and act. In your private time, think about ways to clear away other influences that hinder your relationship to God. Think about the benefits that could come to you as you put Jesus first in your life. Remember that you alone live your life and that no one else can make decisions for you.

11

Obedience By Choice

GROUP LIFE

Growing Together—Praying for Each Other

One necessary reason for prayer is because the world is involved in a controversy between God and Satan. Satan desires to separate the people of this earth from God. This separation results in unhappiness now and ultimately, the loss of eternal life. Prayer strengthens your relationship with God.

Jesus demonstrated the need of prayer in the Garden of Gethsemane prior to His crucifixion. He agonized with God the Father concerning His need of divine strength. He also asked His disciples to pray with Him and for one another. Praying for others is called intercessory prayer. Your group members need to pray for one another during the week. Prayer is not a sign of weakness—even Jesus needed prayer.

Sharing Life

It is true that Christians have difficult times, but Jesus has promised us strength for the negative times. Share with your group what trait you want to develop through the strength Jesus provides. Examples: patience, more kindness, slowness to become angry, etc.

SCRIPTURE AND LIFE

WHAT JESUS SAID ABOUT LAW AND GRACE

"Do not think that I came to destroy the Law or the Prophets. I did not come to destroy but to fulfill."—Matthew 5:17

As you study, be thinking about the LifeQuest questions:

■ What does this topic tell me about God?

■ What difference does this topic make in my daily life?

■ How does this topic help me in my relationship with Jesus?

It is a discussion that confuses some and clarifies the Scriptures for others. It is a discussion that has been with mankind for many years. The discussion? The relationship between law and grace in the Bible.

The reason for the discussion? Several points of view exist, some of which follow:

1. Man is saved by grace, not law, so man does not have to keep the law (Ephesians 2:8, 9).
2. When Jesus died on the cross, the law was blotted out by His death. It is therefore no longer binding on Christians.
3. Matthew 5:17-19 is very clear that Jesus did not come to "destroy" (end) the law, but to demonstrate how to live it ("fulfill" it) in one's life.
4. 1 John 2:3, 4 says that if a person knows or loves God, he or she will "keep the law." If people say they love God and don't keep the law, they are lying!
5. Revelation 14:12 explicitly states that Christians should keep or obey the commandments.

Do you understand the issue? Some say that the Bible gives them permission not to keep the law of God. Others say obedience is necessary for salvation. Still others state that salvation is a free gift and that obedience to God's law is a natural outgrowth of one's love for Him.

The interesting part of the entire discussion emerges when one asks the question, "Which part of God's law is it OK not to obey?" Think about it—do you, or does society, want people to steal, lie, disregard their marriage vows, or tolerate dishonoring of parents? Of course not! Then why do we have the confusion?

The issue focuses on one's understanding about the use of the word *law* in the Bible.

❑   The law, in general, refers to God's revealed will. Read these Scripture references and write down and discuss what you discover concerning the titles used describing God's law. Exodus 34:28; Daniel 9:11; Nehemiah 9:13, 14; Luke 24:44.

_____

_____

A study of the Old Testament reveals that the Bible refers to God's law in a general sense and also divides it into several major categories, such as: (1) the Ten Commandment law, (2) the rest of the law given to Moses, and (3) additional instruction given through the prophets.

❑   The following texts discuss the Ten Commandment law and other laws given to Moses. Information is given concerning who spoke the laws, how they were written, where the laws were stored, the purpose of the laws, etc. Read these texts for informational purposes. You may have questions to discuss, and you may not. Write down pertinent information and discuss any questions or thoughts that come to mind: Exodus 20:1-3, 22, 23; Exodus 24:3, 4; Deuteronomy 31:9, 24-26; 10:1, 2, 12-22. _____

_____

_____

The content of "Moses' Law"—the rest of the law that he wrote in a book and placed in a pocket on the side of the ark (the Ten Commandments on stone were inside the ark)—is found following Exodus 20:1-17 and in the books of Leviticus, Numbers, and Deuteronomy. These laws deal with ceremonies, sacrifices, feast days, ceremonial sabbath days, civil laws governing Israel, health and sanitary laws, etc. If you are not familiar with these chapters, you can read them at your leisure. A study of these chapters reveals that the Ten Commandment law primarily deals with moral precepts.Some of the other laws point to the coming Saviour who would save people from their sin. Other laws were in the form of instructions which applied God's principles to daily living.

In addition to these laws given to Moses, God gave instruction to other prophets. The instruction given to Moses and the other prophets was communicated to God's people and is recorded throughout the Bible.

❑ Read the following texts and discuss the characteristics of God's law: Psalm 19:7-11; Matthew 5:17-19; Matthew 22:36-40. For example, what do the texts say concerning the purpose of God's law? When does it cease to exist? What does the law do for Christians? How does each text assist your understanding of the law?_____

_____

How does God's law make you feel?

___Frustrated—I can't keep it.
___Happy—I know it brings me the best in life.
___Angry—I don't like being told what to do.
___Fearful—I am afraid I can't keep it and will be eternally lost.
___Peaceful—Jesus kept the law perfectly for me.
___Other _____

❑ Read the following texts and form a statement describing the importance and/or relationship of both grace and commandment-keeping. Romans 3:20, 27-31; Romans 7:7; Ephesians 2:8-10; 1 John 2:3-11.

_____

_____

❑ What is the relationship of the mirror and the law in James 1:21-27?_____

James calls the law "the perfect law of liberty." What does He mean?

_____

❏ What is God's desire for all Christians? Share what the following texts mean to you: Hebrews 8:10; 10:15-17._____

_____

❏ If salvation is a free gift, yet God's commandments are still binding, a) discuss how grace and law applies to the Christian's life, and b) indicate which of the following examples helps you to explain law and grace?

___marriage   ___court and judge
___parent/child relationship   ___other_____
___Declaration of Independence

❏ LIFEQUEST—Thoughtfully review these questions:
  ■ What does this topic tell me about God?
  ■ What difference does this topic make in my daily life?
  ■ How does this topic help me in my relationship with Jesus?

APPLICATION TO LIFE

Real Life

Frank had been periodically studying for two years the topic of the relationship between law and grace. The reason for his interest was that he had been taught that a person was saved by grace—and that the law was not binding upon a Christian. Frank was puzzled. He agreed that a person was saved by grace and not by obedience. It was also true that Jesus covered a sinner's sins so they were not held against him as a penalty. But why did Frank find some Christians saying that while some of God's commands were no longer in effect, others were? This seemed contradictory.

As Frank studied, he discovered that in the book of Romans the apostle Paul dealt with the issue of law and grace and summarized it nicely. Paul says in Romans 3:31, "Do we then make void the law through faith? Certainly not! On the contrary, we establish the law."

Studying further, Frank discovered that a Christian is saved by the grace of Jesus. A person is free from the law (that is, from its penalty, because Jesus has covered all confessed sins). But a person is no more free to break God's law than to break the laws of the country. If a judge pardons someone, that does not give that person permission to break the law again! In the same sense, the forgiveness of Jesus does not void the Christian's responsibility to the covenant relationship of the law of God. As Frank studied, he was convinced of the balance of law and grace. The two go together and cannot be separated.

Your Turn

Frank's experience is common to many people studying the subject of law and grace for the first time. Many in life want the most possible with the least amount of responsibility. If some people can have the gift of salvation, yet not have to be concerned with the commands of scripture, they get excited. This is essentially the same as wanting the benefits of a relationship without the commitment that goes with it.

Check the statements that most closely reflect your current feelings. (These are for personal reflection, not group discussion.)

____I still have some unanswered questions regarding the topic of law and grace. I need more study.

____I believe I have adequate information on the topic of law and grace and have a clear understanding of it.

____It is my plan to accept the free gift of salvation and to fully follow the commandments and teachings of the Bible.

____Other_____

Alone With God

As you wake up each morning and begin your day, take time once again to commit your life to God. Ask Him for strength and victory over the temptations and personal struggles you face. Through trust in divine power, victory will be yours.

12

A Day With the Son

GROUP LIFE

Growing Together—the Holy Spirit and the Christian

Jesus was sitting with His disciples following a communion service in an upstairs room. As He talked to them about His coming death and resurrection, He shared a concept that was difficult for them to comprehend. Jesus told them that it was necessary for Him to return to heaven so the third member of the Godhead, the Holy Spirit, would come to them. Part of the work of the Spirit is to assist people in living their daily lives and to guide each person who desires to understand the Bible.

Each member of a Bible study group who desires to grow in his or her relationship with Jesus and to understand the truth found in the Bible will discover benefit in asking God's guidance, available through the Holy Spirit.

Sharing Life

Everyone needs rest. Jesus, in Mark 6:31, told His disciples they needed a break. Share what you like to do in your leisure time.

SCRIPTURE AND LIFE

> ## WHAT JESUS SAID ABOUT THE SABBATH
>
> "And He said to them, 'The Sabbath was made for man, and not man for the Sabbath. Therefore the Son of Man is also Lord of the Sabbath.'"—Mark 2:27, 28
>
> *As you study, be thinking about the LifeQuest questions:*
> - What does this topic tell me about God?
> - What difference does this topic make in my daily life?
> - How does this topic help me in my relationship with Jesus?

Differences of opinion exist among Christians concerning which day of the week is the Sabbath—the day of worship. Some will tell you that Sunday is the Sabbath; others that it is Saturday. And some will state that God doesn't care on which day one worships, as long as one day in seven is recognized as the Sabbath. This subject is important, because the message of Revelation 14, which prepares the world for Christ's second coming, says to "worship" God the Creator, for "the hour of his judgment is come."

To understand what God says about worshiping on the Sabbath, let's do a brief survey of several key scriptures, beginning with Genesis.

❑ A previous study was on the days of creation. Review those six days in Genesis 1. Then read Genesis 2:1-3. Discuss the significant events that occurred concerning the seventh day of creation week.

◆ Why do you think God rested, and what does it mean for God to rest?_____

_____

◆ How is a "blessed," "sanctified," or "holy" day different from the other six days?_____

_____

❑ Years later, God reiterated the significance of the seventh day

when the children of Israel were hungry in the desert. Read
Exodus 16:4, 5, 21-31. Why did God not rain food from heaven
on the seventh day?

___God needed rest from His work in providing manna
___The Israelites needed rest
___The seventh day was special to God
___Other _____

◆   Verse 26 calls the seventh day the Sabbath. What does the
word *Sabbath* mean? (Look it up in a dictionary.)

_____

◆   Verses 27-30 indicate a refusal to listen to God. Why was God
adamant about the need for resting on the seventh day?

___Legalism
___It had to do with the relationship of God to Israel
___It was a holy day
___Other _____

❑   A few chapters later, in Exodus 20:8-11, God writes the Sabbath
commandment in stone as part of the Ten Commandments. Read
these verses and list any points concerning the Sabbath you have
not discovered in the previous two passages.

_____
_____

Why did God give the Sabbath to man? What is the purpose of the
Sabbath?_____

❑   A significant passage of scripture about the Sabbath and Jesus is
in Luke 23:50 through 24:1-8. Read these verses, noting what is
stated concerning three of the days of the week and the significance and/or events which occurred on each of the days. _____

_____

◆   What are these three days called today in celebrating Easter weekend? (A calendar could be helpful)

_____Friday

_____Saturday

_____Sunday

❏   Following the death of Jesus, the apostle Paul worshiped on the seventh day. Read Acts 17:1-4 and Acts 13:42-52. Discuss any points you find significant._____

_____

(Additional seventh-day and Sabbath passages: Mark 2:27, 28; Matthew 12:9-14; Nehemiah 13:15-22; Isaiah 58:13, 14.)

❏   The next study guide will deal with the meaning of the Sabbath; however, briefly discuss the LifeQuest questions to summarize the reason for the Sabbath in one's daily life.

❏   LIFEQUEST—Thoughtfully review these questions:

■ What does this topic tell me about God?

■ What difference does this topic make in my daily life?

■ How does this topic help me in my relationship with Jesus?

APPLICATION TO LIFE

Real Life

Linda thought that those who believed that the seventh day of the week (Saturday) was holy were legalists. She had grown up worshipping God on Sunday. It was her family's practice to go shopping or to work in the yard after church each week. However, she discovered that some Christians had a different view. As Linda dealt with the subject, a friend provided her with some thoughts to consider.

Her friend shared with her that God has said no one is to work on the Sabbath (Exodus 20:8-11). Even if a person believed the Sabbath to be a different day than Saturday, the principle would be the same—the day was not to be a work day. If everyone obeyed God, only necessary work for humanitarian reasons would be done. Linda's friend shared with her that in her own relationship with Jesus, this was not legalism but a highlight of her week.

The purpose of the Sabbath includes physical rest as well as a special time with Jesus. It is like a husband and wife having an anniversary date every week. They want their special time not be interrupted by outside distractions.

As Linda contemplated what she was learning, she realized that the Sabbath was only legalism if a person was not in love with Jesus.

Your Turn

Maybe you are struggling with the issue of what it means to "remember the Sabbath day"? Keep in mind that no one should make your decisions about Sabbath keeping for you. Make your decisions based upon principle. Ask yourself whether a particular event or activity assists or detracts from your time with Jesus.

Check the statements that most closely reflect your current feelings. (These are for personal reflection, not group discussion.)

___I need additional information so I can continue to study more about the Sabbath.

___I understand why some Christians are willing to be different from the rest of the world and keep the seventh-day Sabbath.

___I desire to worship on the Sabbath.

___Other_____

Alone With God

If you have decided to begin worshiping on the Sabbath, ask your leader or another group member if you can go to church with him or her. Also ask if you can spend a Sabbath with someone so you can better understand what they do on the Sabbath. Another suggestion would be for as many group members whose schedules will permit it to spend a Sabbath together.

13

God's Sabbath—Its Meaning

GROUP LIFE

Growing Together—Community in Small Group Life

The key ingredients found in a Bible study group during the week should also be found in the life of the church as it worships on the Sabbath. Of course, the opportunity for these elements to function may vary, but nonetheless, they will be present. These ingredients include fellowship, worship, Bible study, and outreach.

Sharing Life

The New Testament Gospels portray a group of disciples growing daily in learning about Jesus. Share how your Bible study group has (a) assisted you in your daily life or (b) a way you hope they will assist you in the future.

SCRIPTURE AND LIFE

WHAT JESUS SAID ABOUT THE SABBATH

"What man is there among you who has one sheep, and if it falls into a pit on the Sabbath, will not lay hold of it and lift it out? "Of how much more value then is a man than a sheep? Therefore it is lawful to do good on the Sabbath."—Matthew 12:11, 12

As you study, be thinking about the LifeQuest questions:
■ What does this topic tell me about God?
■ What difference does this topic make in my daily life?
■ How does this topic help me in my relationship with Jesus?

God gave the Sabbath to Christians for many reasons. These reasons have a deep significance for the relationship of God to His people. Read the following texts and discuss seven of the numerous reasons given for the Sabbath.

❑ **A Memorial of Creation.** Exodus 20:11.
Why is it important to recognize God as Creator of the world once a week? What difference does it make in one's daily life?

_____

❑ **A Symbol of Redemption (Freedom).** Deuteronomy 5:15.
The Sabbath was a symbol of Israel's deliverance from slavery in Egypt. In what ways can the Sabbath symbolize freedom for Christians today? Mark the following answer which is most significant to you.

___freedom from sin   ___freedom from guilt
___freedom from everyday   ___other_____
    problems
___freedom from social inequality

❑ **A Sign of Sanctification.** Exodus 31:13; Ezekiel 20:20.

Define sanctification. How is one sanctified? Hebrews 13:12.

❑ **A Sign of Loyalty.** Revelation 14:9-12. (Verse 12 is key.)
God's people today have a symbol of their relationship to Him in
the Sabbath. Discuss the Sabbath as a sign of loyalty.

❑ **A Time of Fellowship (Relationship).** Mark 2:27, 28.
Man was created in God's image (Genesis 1:26) to interact with
Him. How does the Sabbath help develop a relationship with
God? With friends? With family?_____

❑ **A Symbol of Righteousness By Faith.** 1 Peter 2:21-24. Even
though this text does not directly mention the Sabbath, but refers
to "holy commandment," discuss the questions that follow:

Define righteousness. Define faith._____

Discuss how the meaning of the Sabbath and the meaning of
righteousness by faith are related to one another.

❑ **A Symbol of Resting in Christ.** Genesis 2:2; Hebrews 4:9, 10.
Discuss the importance of physical and spiritual rest to the
Christian._____

The Sabbath/Sunday Question

The question which naturally comes to mind regarding the Sabbath
is, Why do most Christians attend church on Sunday, the first day of the
week, rather than Saturday, the seventh day of the week? Numerous texts
mention the seventh day in the Bible. Interestingly, however, only seven
New Testament references mention the first day of the week (Sunday).

❑ Look up each of these texts and discuss any significance they

have in regard to worshiping on Sunday or Sunday being the
Sabbath. Matt. 28:1; Mark 16:1, 2; Mark 16:9; Luke 24:1; John
20:1; John 20:19; Acts 20:7, 8 _____

_____

The change in observing the Sabbath from Saturday to Sunday took
place gradually throughout history. During the time of Jesus' life on this
earth, Rome was the leading empire of the world. Rome's reign began in
168 B.C. and continued for six centuries. It was during the reign of the
Roman Empire that the change took place.

There is no evidence of Christian weekly Sunday worship before
the second century. However, by the middle of that century, some Christians worshiped on Sunday. The Church of Rome—the official church
of the Roman empire—led in the trend toward Sunday worship. In response to anti-Jewish sentiments and converted pagans, some practices
in common with the Jews (including Saturday as the Sabbath) were
dropped, and Rome moved toward exclusive observance of Sunday.

The first Sunday observance law was issued by the Roman emperor
Constantine on March 7, A.D. 321. A portion of the law read, "On the
venerable Day of the Sun let the magistrates and people residing in cit-
ies rest, and let all workshops be closed. In the country however, persons engaging in agriculture may freely and lawfully continue their pur-
suits."—*History of the Christian Church,* 5th ed. Schaff, vol. 3, p. 380,
note 1.

The Council of Laodicea (A.D. 364) issued the first ecclesiastical
(or church) Sunday Law. It stipulated that Christians should honor Sunday and if possible not work on that day. The law further stated that it
was not wrong for Christians to work on Saturday. (*SDA Bible Student's
Source Book*, rev. ed. p. 885.)

In A.D. 538, the Third Council of Orleans stated that on Sunday,
even agricultural work should not be done, so that Christians could attend church. (*God Cares*, vol.1, Maxwell.) As the centuries continued to
march onward, Sunday observance became an anchored tradition for
Catholics and Protestants. Eventually, some tried to establish a scriptural basis for the change, but most theologians agree that the change
was man-made and not scriptural.

❏ LIFEQUEST—Thoughtfully review these questions:
   ■ What does this topic tell me about God?
   ■ What difference does this topic make in my daily life?
   ■ How does this topic help me in my relationship with Jesus?

APPLICATION TO LIFE

Real Life

Cheryl accepted Jesus as Lord of her life shortly after her marriage. Cheryl's husband, however, did not follow Cheryl in her acceptance of Jesus. Cheryl's interest took her to a series of prophecy lectures in a church that worshiped on Saturday. During the meetings, she was convinced of the fact that Saturday was the Sabbath of the Bible.

Cheryl was torn between what she had always done and what she felt convicted to do. As she considered her situation, she decided to continue attending church on Sunday and not on Saturday. However, she would do all that was possible not to violate the Saturday Sabbath whenever she was able to do so conveniently.

Your Turn

Serving God sometimes means that a person must make decisions that cause changes in his or her life. When this occurs, God has given promises in the Bible to provide strength and encouragement.

"I can do all things through Christ who strengthens me." Philippians 4:13.

"And we know that all things work together for good to them that love God, to them who are the called according to His purpose." Romans 8:28.

Check the statements that most closely reflect your current feelings.

(The following statements are for personal reflection, not group discussion.)

____I believe the Sabbath is a symbol of my love for God.
____I understand the Bible Sabbath and would like to begin
       keeping it sometime in the future.

___I believe that Saturday is the Sabbath of the Bible, and I choose to worship God on this day.

___I am going to study this subject until I am certain about my answer as to which day of the week is God's Sabbath.

___Other_____

Alone With God

As a member of the group, you have now completed thirteen study guides. As you reflect upon these lessons, if you realize you need more study in certain areas, pray for understanding and talk to your group leader.

A Book Two in this series is available that covers thirteen more vital Bible subjects.